THE ICE CREAM BOOK

by

Shona Crawford Poole
and
Jasper Partington

Contents

This edition first published 1980 by
Octopus Books Limited,
59 Grosvenor, Street, London W.1.

© 1980 Shona Crawford Poole and Jasper Partington

ISBN 0 7064 1138 2

All photographs taken by Jasper Partington.

Produced and printed in Hong Kong by
Mandarin Publishers Limited
22a Westlands Road, Quarry Bay.
Hong Kong.

Frontispiece *From left:* BUTTERSCOTCH *(page 40),* CARAMEL *(page 39)* AND TEA *(page 40)* ICE CREAMS

Weights and Measures

All measurements in the book are given in Metric, Imperial and American.

Measurements in weight in the Imperial and American system are the same. Liquid measurements are different, and the following table shows the equivalents:

Liquid measurements
1 Imperial Pint... 20 fluid ounces
1 American Pint.. 16 fluid ounces
1 American cup .... 8 fluid ounces

Level spoon measurements are used in all the recipes.

Spoon measurements
1 Tablespoon .... 15 ml
1 Teaspoon ....5 ml

Remember that the ingredients column are not interchangeable. Follow only one set of measures.

INTRODUCTION

Recipes for homemade ice creams have been published since the middle of the eighteenth century. But, it was not until the twentieth century, when reliable domestic refrigerators and freezers did away with the need for dripping ice blocks and hand-cranked churning contraptions, that making ice cream at home became a practical proposition.

Why go to the trouble and expense of making ices at home when the factory product is available in family packs from every supermarket and freezer centre? On nutritional grounds alone ices made at home with fresh eggs, milk, cream and fruit, win easily over most commercial products. But the most persuasive argument is, of course, taste. Quite simply, homemade ices are so delicious that you will want to make your favourite recipes again and again.

Ice creams are based on an egg custard or mousse, or simply on cream. They always contain milk or cream.

Sherbets are fairly dense ices based on sweetened fruit juice or purée or on flavoured syrup.

Sorbets are ices based on sweetened fruit juice or purée, or on flavoured syrup, with the addition of uncooked meringue.

Parfaits, mousses and soufflés are similar to ice cream but lighter in texture. They may be frozen without stirring.

No special equipment is needed for any of the recipes which follow. Most of them can be made successfully in the ice-making compartment of any domestic refrigerator. A four-star deep freeze will firm ice cream more quickly than a simple ice-making shelf and is therefore an advantage, but by no means essential. Small sorbetiers, ice cream making machines which stir the mixture as it freezes, are available, and may be useful to cooks who have no time to whisk the mixture once or twice during freezing. They do not, in my experience, make better ices.

The rules for making superb ice cream are few and simple.

Ice creams are best frozen as fast as possible so turn the freezer to its coldest setting at least an hour before placing the ice cream container in the coldest part of the freezer.

Shallow metal containers are more efficient conductors of heat, and therefore cold, than plastic containers and are useful for freezing small quantities of ice cream in a refrigerator. Maximize its limited freezing capacity by pouring a little water on the floor of the freezing compartment just before setting the tray on it.

Custards will curdle if boiled, so cook them in the top of a double boiler if you have difficulty regulating the heat.

Whipped cream is deflated by contact with anything warm, so make sure that custards and purées are really cold, preferably chilled, before adding whipped cream.

Whisking partially frozen ice cream will increase its volume

If a vanilla pod (bean) is not available for flavouring, substitute 2 teaspoons vanilla essence (extract). Add the vanilla to the cold custard. If using vanilla essence (extract) just heat the milk before adding to the egg yolks but do not infuse; add the vanilla to the mixture before freezing.

Ices are whisked during freezing to make them smooth by breaking up large ice crystals and incorporating air into the mixture. An electric beater is useful for this task, but it can also be done by hand. It does not matter if the ice cream melts, it will firm up again. The important thing is to beat the ice cream very thoroughly.

The best time to beat most ices is when the mixture at the sides and bottom of the container is quite firm and the centre is still very soft. If the ice freezes hard before it is beaten, place it in the refrigerator until it is soft enough to whisk.

Freezing times will vary greatly depending on the ingredients in the mixture and the temperature of the freezer. Various ingredients such as alcohol, sugar, fat and gelatine, inhibit freezing in different ways, so recipes containing large amounts of these will take longer to freeze, and will not freeze as hard as other mixtures. All the recipes which follow have been tested in a home freezer. If you are using the ice-making compartment of a refrigerator which has a rating of less than three stars, it may be necessary to reduce the alcohol or sugar content of some of the sherbet and sorbet recipes.

Ices are best covered during freezing, and should always be covered for storage.

Nearly all ices should be ripened in the main compartment of the refrigerator before serving. This brings out the full flavour of the ice and softens it just enough to make serving easy. Ripening times vary from ten minutes to over an hour depending on the quantity, the shape of the container, the temperature of the freezer it has been stored in, and the ingredients in the ice. An average time is 30 to 40 minutes for a plastic container holding 1 litre/1 ³/₄ pints/4 ¹/₄ cups, and 10 to 15 minutes for ices frozen in individual servings.

Unless otherwise stated, all recipes in this book make approximately 1 litre/1 ³/₄ pints/4 ¹/₄ cups.

CLASSIC TASTES

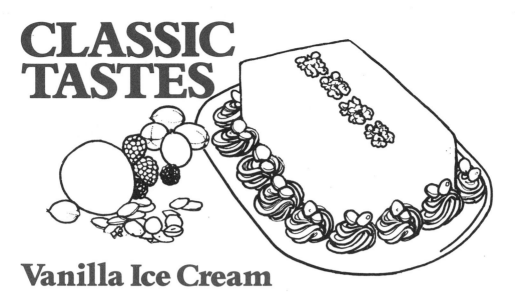

Vanilla Ice Cream

METRIC/IMPERIAL	AMERICAN
300 ml/½ pint milk	*1¼ cups milk*
10 cm/4 inch piece vanilla pod or	*4 inch piece vanilla bean or*
* 2 teaspoons vanilla essence*	* 2 teaspoons vanilla extract*
4 egg yolks	*4 egg yolks*
100 g/4 oz caster sugar	*½ cup superfine sugar*
pinch of salt	*pinch of salt*
300 ml/½ pint double cream	*1¼ cups heavy cream*
2 tablespoons iced water	*2 tablespoons iced water*

Turn the freezer to the coldest setting about 1 hour before starting. Slowly heat the milk and the vanilla pod (bean), halved lengthwise. When almost boiling, remove the pan from the heat and set aside to infuse for about 20 minutes.

Beat the egg yolks, sugar and salt together until the mixture is very pale and the whisk leaves a trail. Slowly add the strained warm milk, whisking all the time. Return the mixture to the pan and cook over a very low heat, stirring constantly, until the custard is thick enough to coat the back of a wooden spoon. Set aside to cool, stirring occasionally. Chill the custard. Add the vanilla essence (extract) if using.

Whip the cream with the iced water until it forms soft peaks. Combine the cream with the cold custard and beat lightly together. Pour into suitable freezer trays and still-freeze. When the mixture is half frozen, remove and beat thoroughly to break down the ice crystals. Return to the freezer trays and refreeze. If liked, beat again when half frozen. Do not worry if the mixture melts during the beating, it will freeze again. After the mixture has frozen, return the freezer or refrigerator to its usual temperature.

To serve, take from the freezer about 30 minutes before serving and put in the refrigerator to allow the ice cream to soften slightly.

French Vanilla Ice Cream

METRIC/IMPERIAL	AMERICAN
175 ml/6 fl oz sweetened condensed milk	3/4 cup sweetened condensed milk
450 ml/3/4 pint double cream	2 cups heavy cream
1 teaspoon vanilla essence	1 teaspoon vanilla extract

Combine all the ingredients in a large bowl and chill in the refrigerator for 30 minutes. Whisk the mixture until it forms stiff peaks. Spoon into freezer containers and still-freeze. It is not necessary to whisk during the freezing.

Quick and Easy Vanilla Ice Cream

METRIC/IMPERIAL	AMERICAN
750 ml/1 1/4 pints milk	3 cups milk
10 cm/4 inch piece vanilla pod or 1-2 teaspoons vanilla essence	4 inch piece vanilla bean or 1-2 teaspoons vanilla extract
6 egg yolks	6 egg yolks
275 g/10 oz caster sugar	1 1/4 cups superfine sugar
pinch of salt	pinch of salt

Slowly heat the milk and vanilla pod (bean), halved lengthwise. When almost boiling, remove the pan from the heat and set aside to infuse for about 20 minutes.

Beat the egg yolks, sugar and salt together, until the mixture is very pale and the whisk leaves a trail. Slowly add the strained warm milk, whisking all the time. Return the mixture to the pan and cook over a very low heat, stirring constantly, until the custard is thick enough to coat the back of a wooden spoon. Set the custard aside and stir it occasionally while it cools.

Add the vanilla essence (extract), if using.

Pour into freezer trays and still-freeze, whisking the mixture once or twice during freezing.

From rear left: VANILLA ICE CREAM *(page 11)*, WITH CHOCOLATE SAUCE *(page 78)*, FRENCH VANILLA ICE CREAM, QUICK AND EASY VANILLA ICE CREAM with wafers and VANILLA ICE CREAM WITHOUT EGGS *(page 14)*

Vanilla Ice Cream Without Eggs

METRIC/IMPERIAL	AMERICAN
600 ml/1 pint milk	2¹/2 cups milk
10 cm/4 inch piece vanilla pod or	4 inch piece vanilla bean or
1-2 teaspoons vanilla essence	1-2 teaspoons vanilla extract
450 ml/³/4 pint double cream	2 cups heavy cream
100 g/4 oz granulated sugar	¹/2 cup sugar
pinch of salt	pinch of salt
2 tablespoons cornflour	2 tablespoons cornstarch

Set aside about 4 tablespoons/¹/4 cup of the milk. Put the remaining milk in a pan with the vanilla pod (bean), halved lengthwise. Bring the milk almost to the boil then remove from the heat. Set aside to infuse for about 20 minutes.

Strain the flavoured milk and return it to the pan with the cream, sugar and salt. Bring the mixture to the boil then lower the heat. Blend the cornflour (cornstarch) with the reserved milk and stir it into the hot milk mixture. Cook over a low heat for a minute or two after it thickens, stirring constantly.

Transfer the custard to a bowl and stir often as it cools, to prevent a thick skin forming. Add the vanilla essence (extract), if using. Pour into freezer trays and still freeze, whisking once or twice during freezing.

Tutti Frutti Ice Cream

METRIC/IMPERIAL	AMERICAN
50 g/2 oz sultanas	¹/3 cup seedless white raisins
50 g/2 oz glacé cherries, chopped	¹/4 cup chopped candied cherries
50 g/2 oz angelica, chopped	¹/4 cup chopped angelica
4 tablespoons Kirsch	¹/4 cup Kirsch
1 litre/1³/4 pints Vanilla Ice Cream	4¹/4 cups Vanilla Ice Cream
(see pages 11-14)	(see pages 11-14)

Use ice cream that has been made to the half-frozen state or softened already made ice cream.

Mix the sultanas (seedless white raisins), cherries and angelica in a small bowl and pour the Kirsch over them. Cover and set aside to marinate for at least an hour.

Drain the fruit and combine it with the half-frozen or softened ice cream. Mix well to distribute the fruit evenly throughout the mixture. Return to the freezer trays and still-freeze until firm.
Makes about 1.2 litres/2 pints/5 cups

Variation:
Other fruits may be used in place of the sultanas (white raisins), cherries or angelica. Soak the fruit in liqueur or fruit syrup.

Praline Ice Cream

Caramelized nuts are a classic flavour in cake and pudding making. For the praline use toasted almonds, walnuts, hazelnuts, pistachios or peanuts.

METRIC/IMPERIAL
6 egg yolks
275 g/10 oz caster sugar
750 ml/1 ¼ pints milk
50 g/2 oz blanched almonds
1 teaspoon vanilla essence

AMERICAN
6 egg yolks
1 ¼ cups superfine sugar
3 cups milk
½ cup blanched almonds
1 teaspoon vanilla extract

Put the egg yolks in a pan with 225 g/8 oz/1 cup of the sugar and beat until the mixture is very pale and the whisk leaves a trail. Slowly add the milk, whisking all the time.

Cook the mixture over a low heat stirring constantly, until the custard is thick enough to coat the back of a wooden spoon. Set the custard aside and stir it occasionally while it cools.

Spread the blanched almonds on a baking sheet and toast them in a preheated moderate oven (160°C/325°F, Gas Mark 3) for about 10 minutes, or until they are well browned. Spread the almonds on a sheet of greased foil.

Put the remaining sugar in a small, heavy based pan. Cook over a low heat until the sugar has melted and turned a rich golden brown. Pour the caramel over the toasted almonds and set the mixture aside to cool.

Crush the praline by pounding it in a mortar, or process in a food processer to crumb sized chips and powder.

Combine the cold custard with the crushed praline and vanilla and mix them well together. Pour into freezer trays and still-freeze, whisking the mixture once or twice during freezing.

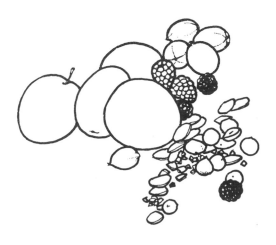

Almond Ice Cream

For the best flavour, use good quality almonds, freshly shelled, and if you can buy them, include 4 bitter almonds.

METRIC/IMPERIAL	AMERICAN
750 ml/1 ¼ pints milk	*3 cups milk*
100 g/4 oz ground almonds	*1 cup ground almonds*
6 egg yolks	*6 egg yolks*
275 g/10 oz caster sugar	*1 ¼ cups superfine sugar*
pinch of salt	*pinch of salt*

Bring the milk to the boil, simmer for a minute then remove from the heat. Stir in the ground almonds and set the mixture aside to infuse for about 30 minutes. Strain through a fine sieve.

Beat the egg yolks, sugar and salt together until the mixture is very pale and the whisk leaves a trail. Slowly add the warm, flavoured milk, whisking all the time. Return the mixture to the pan and cook over a very low heat, stirring constantly, until the custard is thick enough to coat the back of a wooden spoon. Set the custard aside and stir it occasionally while it cools. Pour into freezer trays and still-freeze, whisking the mixture once or twice during freezing.

Hazlenut Ice Cream

METRIC/IMPERIAL	AMERICAN
100 g/4 oz shelled hazelnuts	*¾ cup shelled hazelnuts*
4 egg yolks	*4 egg yolks*
175 g/6 oz caster sugar	*¾ cup superfine sugar*
300 ml/½ pint milk	*1 ¼ cups milk*
250 ml/8 fl oz double cream	*1 cup heavy cream*
2 tablespoons iced water	*2 tablespoons iced water*

Spread the hazelnuts on a baking sheet and roast in a preheated moderate oven (160°C/325°F, Gas Mark 3) for about 15 minutes, or until the centres are a pale biscuit colour. Cool the nuts, rub off the skins and grind or pound the kernels.

Beat the egg yolks and sugar together until the mixture is very pale and the whisk leaves a trail. Add the milk and pour into a pan. Cook over a very low heat, stirring constantly, until the custard is thick enough to coat the back of a wooden spoon. Set the custard aside and stir it occasionally while it cools. Chill.

Whip the cream with the iced water until it forms soft peaks. Combine the cold custard with the hazelnuts and whipped cream and beat them lightly together. Pour into freezer trays and still-freeze, whisking the mixture once or twice during freezing.

Left rear to front: ALMOND, WALNUT *(page 18)*, PISTACHIO *(page 18)*, HAZLENUT AND PRALINE *(page 15)* ICE CREAMS

Walnut Ice Cream

METRIC/IMPERIAL
3 egg yolks
225 g/8 oz soft brown sugar
pinch of salt
300 ml/½ pint milk
250 ml/8 fl oz double cream
2 tablespoons iced water
50 g/2 oz shelled walnuts, chopped
4 tablespoons sweet sherry

AMERICAN
3 egg yolks
1⅓ cups soft brown sugar
pinch of salt
1¼ cups milk
1 cup heavy cream
2 tablespoons iced water
½ cup shelled walnuts, chopped
¼ cup sweet sherry

Beat the egg yolks, sugar and salt together until the mixture is light and spongy. Slowly add the milk, whisking all the time. Pour into a saucepan.

Cook the mixture over a low heat, stirring constantly, until the custard is thick enough to coat the back of a wooden spoon. Set the custard aside and stir it occasionally while it cools. Chill.

Whip the cream with the iced water until it forms soft peaks. Combine the cold custard with the whipped cream, walnuts and sherry and beat them lightly together. Pour into freezer trays and still-freeze, whisking once or twice during freezing.

Pistachio Ice Cream

METRIC/IMPERIAL
750 ml/1¼ pints milk
100 g/4 oz unsalted shelled
  pistachios, finely ground
6 egg yolks
275 g/10 oz caster sugar
pinch of salt
½ teaspoon almond essence
green food colouring (optional)

AMERICAN
3 cups milk
1 cup unsalted shelled pistachios,
  finely ground
6 egg yolks
1¼ cups superfine sugar
pinch of salt
½ teaspoon almond extract
green food coloring (optional)

Bring the milk to the boil, simmer for 1 minute and remove from the heat. Stir in the ground pistachios and set the mixture aside to infuse for about 30 minutes. Strain it through a fine sieve.

Beat the egg yolks, sugar and salt together until the mixture is very pale and the whisk leaves a trail. Slowly add the warm, flavoured milk, whisking all the time. Return the mixture to the pan and cook over a very low heat, stirring constantly, until the custard is thick enough to coat the back of a wooden spoon. Set the custard aside and stir it occasionally as it cools.

Add the almond essence (extract) to the cool custard, and the food colouring, if using. Stir well. Pour into freezer trays and still-freeze, whisking the mixture once or twice during freezing.

FRUIT ICES

Blackcurrant Sorbet

METRIC/IMPERIAL	AMERICAN
450 g/1 lb blackcurrants	4 cups blackcurrants
juice of 2 oranges	juice of 2 oranges
150 g/6 oz caster sugar	¾ cup superfine sugar
2 egg whites	2 egg whites
2 tablespoons icing sugar	2 tablespoons confectioners' sugar

Top and tail the blackcurrants. Purée the fruit by processing it quickly in a blender, or pressing through a sieve. Combine the strained purée with the orange juice and sugar. Stir from time to time until the sugar has completely dissolved. Pour into freezer trays and still-freeze until slushy.

Whisk the egg whites until foamy, add the icing (confectioners') sugar, and continue whisking until the meringue holds stiff peaks. Tip the half-frozen ice into a chilled bowl and whisk thoroughly. Add the meringue and beat lightly together. Return to the freezer trays and still-freeze. Whisk the mixture once more during freezing, if necessary.

Redcurrant Sherbet

METRIC/IMPERIAL	AMERICAN
1 kg/2 lb redcurrants	8 cups of redcurrants
juice of 1 orange	juice of 1 orange
225 g/8 oz caster sugar	1 cup superfine sugar

Top and tail the redcurrants. Purée the fruit by processing it in a blender or pressing through a sieve. Combine the strained purée with the orange juice and sugar. Stir from time to time until the sugar has completely dissolved. Pour into freezer trays and still-freeze, whisking once or twice during freezing.

Orange Sorbet

METRIC/IMPERIAL	AMERICAN
5 oranges	5 oranges
1 lemon	1 lemon
175 g/6 oz granulated sugar	3/4 cup sugar
300 ml/1/2 pint water	1 1/4 cups water
2 egg whites	2 egg whites
2 tablespoons icing sugar	2 tablespoons confectioners' sugar

Cut the peel from the oranges and lemon using a very sharp knife. Take care not to include any of the bitter white pith. Put the peel in a pan with the sugar and water and slowly heat the mixture until the sugar has dissolved completely. Raise the heat and boil the syrup for 5 minutes then set it aside to cool.

Squeeze the juice from the fruit. Combine the cold syrup with the juice and strain the mixture. Pour into freezer trays and still-freeze until slushy.

Beat the egg whites until foamy, add the icing sugar and continue beating until the meringue holds stiff peaks.

Tip the half-frozen ice into a chilled bowl. Add the meringue and beat the mixture until it is well combined. Return to the freezer trays and still-freeze, whisking the mixture once or twice during freezing.

Apricot Sorbet

METRIC/IMPERIAL	AMERICAN
225 g/8 oz dried apricots	1 1/2 cups dried apricots
600 ml/1 pint water	2 1/2 cups water
100 g/4 oz granulated sugar	1/2 cup sugar
juice of 2 lemons	juice of 2 lemons
2 egg whites	2 egg whites
2 tablespoons icing sugar	2 tablespoons confectioners' sugar

Put the apricots and water in a pan, cover and soak for at least an hour.

Add the granulated sugar to the apricots and bring to the boil. Lower the heat and simmer gently for about 10 minutes or until the apricots are tender. Set aside until cold. Purée the apricots and syrup by processing them in a blender or pressing through a sieve. Stir in the lemon juice. Pour into freezer trays and still-freeze until slushy.

Beat the egg whites until foamy, add the icing (confectioners') sugar and continue beating until the meringue holds stiff peaks.

Tip the half-frozen ice into a chilled bowl. Add the meringue and beat the mixture until it is smooth and well blended. Return to the freezer trays and still-freeze. Whisk once more during freezing.

From left: APRICOT, BLACKCURRANT (page 19), LEMON (page 22) AND ORANGE SORBETS, REDCURRANT (page 19) AND TANGERINE SHERBETS (page 22)

Lemon Sorbet

METRIC/IMPERIAL	AMERICAN
4 lemons	4 lemons
1 orange	1 orange
450 ml/³⁄4 pint water	2 cups water
225 g/8 oz granulated sugar	1 cup sugar
2 egg whites	2 egg whites
2 tablespoons icing sugar	2 tablespoons confectioners' sugar

Cut the peel from the lemons and orange using a very sharp knife; take care not to include any of the pith. Put the peel in a pan with the water and sugar and slowly heat until the sugar has dissolved completely. Raise the heat and boil the syrup for 5 minutes then set it aside to cool.

Squeeze the juice from the fruit. Combine the syrup with the juice and strain the mixture. Pour into freezer trays and still-freeze until slushy.

Beat the egg whites until foamy, add the icing (confectioners') sugar and continue beating until the meringue holds stiff peaks.

Tip the partially frozen ice into a chilled bowl. Add the meringue and beat the mixture until it is well blended. Return to the freezer trays and still-freeze, whisking the mixture once more during freezing.

Tangerine Sherbet

Fresh fruit juice and sugar make a dense, sweet sherbet which freezes smoothly without stirring. Whisking the mixture during freezing lightens the ice and increases its volume. This quantity can be doubled by combining the partially frozen and beaten mixture with a meringue of 2 egg whites and 2 tablespoons of icing (confectioners') sugar.

METRIC/IMPERIAL	AMERICAN
750 g/1 ¹⁄2 lb tangerines	1 ¹⁄2 lb tangerines
juice of 1 lemon	juice of 1 lemon
225 g/8 oz caster sugar	1 cup superfine sugar

Squeeze and strain the juice from the tangerines and combine it with the lemon juice and sugar. Stir from time to time until the sugar has dissolved completely. Pour the mixture into feeezer trays and still-freeze.
Makes at least 600 ml/1 pint/2¹⁄2 cups

Variation:
If tangerines are not in season, oranges can be substituted.

Iced Strawberry Mousse

METRIC/IMPERIAL	AMERICAN
350 g/12 oz strawberries	2½ cups strawberries
100 g/4 oz granulated sugar	½ cup sugar
2 eggs, separated	2 eggs, separated
100 g/4 oz icing sugar	1 cup confectioners' sugar
150 ml/¼ pint double cream	⅔ cup heavy cream
1 tablespoon iced water	1 tablespoon iced water

Hull, wash and dry the strawberries. Rub them through a sieve, or process them quickly in a blender and strain the purée. Add the granulated sugar and refrigerate the purée for at least an hour.

Beat the egg yolks lightly with 50 g/2 oz/½ cup of the icing (confectioners') sugar. Set the bowl over a pan of just simmering water and continue beating. When the mixture is lukewarm, take the bowl off the heat and continue beating until the egg mousse is cool and has tripled its original volume. Chill.

Whisk the egg whites in another bowl until foamy. Add the remaining icing (confectioners') sugar and continue beating until the meringue holds stiff peaks.

Whip the cream with the iced water until it forms soft peaks. Combine the chilled strawberry purée and egg mousse. Add the meringue and the whipped cream and beat them lightly together. Pour the mixture into individual dishes or one large bowl and still-freeze, without further beating. Serve with whipped cream or strawberries.

Strawberry Ice Cream

METRIC/IMPERIAL	AMERICAN
350 g/12 oz strawberries, fresh or frozen	2½ cups strawberries, fresh or frozen
75 g/3 oz granulated sugar	⅓ cup sugar
juice of 1 orange	juice of 1 orange
juice of 1 lemon	juice of 1 lemon
3 egg yolks	3 egg yolks
100 g/4 oz icing sugar	1 cup confectioners' sugar
250 ml/8 fl oz double cream	1 cup heavy cream
2 tablespoons iced water	2 tablespoons iced water

Hull, wash and dry the strawberries. Rub them through a sieve, or process them quickly in a blender and strain the purée. Mix the strawberry purée with the granulated sugar, orange and lemon juices, and refrigerate for at least an hour.

Beat the egg yolks lightly with the icing (confectioners') sugar. Set the bowl over a pan of just simmering water and continue beating. When the mixture is lukewarm, take the bowl off the heat and continue beating until the egg mousse is cool and has tripled its original volume. Chill.

Whip the cream with the iced water until it forms soft peaks. Combine the strawberry purée, egg mousse and whipped cream and beat them lightly together. Pour into freezer trays and still-freeze, whisking the mixture once during freezing.

From left: ICED STRAWBERRY MOUSSE *(page 23),* STRAWBERRY SORBET *(page 26),* STRAWBERRY ICE CREAM

Strawberry Sorbet

METRIC/IMPERIAL	AMERICAN
450 g/1 lb strawberries	3 1/4 cups strawberries
225 g/8 oz granulated sugar	1 cup sugar
juice of 1 orange	juice of 1 orange
juice of 1 lemon	juice of 1 lemon
2 egg whites	2 egg whites
2 tablespoons icing sugar	2 tablespoons confectioners' sugar

Hull, wash and dry the strawberries. Rub them through a sieve or process them quickly in a blender, then strain the purée. Mix the purée with the granulated sugar, orange and lemon juices and refrigerate for at least an hour. Pour into freezer trays and still-freeze until slushy.

Beat the egg whites until foamy, add the icing (confectioners') sugar and continue beating until the meringue holds stiff peaks.

Tip the partially frozen ice into a chilled bowl and beat it thoroughly. Add the meringue and beat them lightly together.

Return the mixture to the freezer trays and still-freeze, whisking once more during freezing.

Grapefruit and Mint Sorbet

METRIC/IMPERIAL	AMERICAN
2 large grapefruit	2 large grapefruit
300 ml/1/2 pint water	1 1/4 cups water
225 g/8 oz granulated sugar	1 cup sugar
a handful of fresh mint	a handful of fresh mint
2 egg whites	2 egg whites
2 tablespoons icing sugar	2 tablespoons confectioners' sugar

Finely grate the rind from one of the grapefruit and put in a pan with the water and granulated sugar. Heat the mixture slowly until the sugar has dissolved completely, then raise the heat and boil the syrup for 5 minutes. Add the crushed and roughly chopped mint and set aside until cold.

Squeeze the juice from the grapefruit and strain. Combine the strained syrup with the fruit juice and still-freeze the mixture until slushy.

Beat the egg whites until foamy, add the icing (confectioners') sugar and continue beating until the meringue holds stiff peaks. Tip the partially frozen ice into a chilled bowl and beat it thoroughly. Add the meringue and beat them lightly together. Still-freeze, whisking the mixture once more during freezing.

Tangerine Ice Cream

To freeze the mixture in the fruit shells, scoop out the flesh and chill the shells before spooning or piping in the ice cream after its final beating.

METRIC/IMPERIAL	AMERICAN
4 egg yolks	4 egg yolks
50 g/2 oz icing sugar	1/2 cup confectioners' sugar
juice of 1 lemon	juice of 1 lemon
300 ml/1/2 pint tangerine juice (see note)	1 1/4 cups tangerine juice (see note)
175 g/6 oz caster sugar	3/4 cup superfine sugar
150 ml/1/4 pint double cream	2/3 cup heavy cream
1 tablespoon iced water	1 tablespoon iced water

Beat the egg yolks lightly with the icing (confectioners') sugar. Set the bowl over a pan of just simmering water and continue beating. When the mixture is lukewarm, take the bowl off the heat and continue beating until it is cool and has tripled its original volume. Chill the egg mousse.

Meanwhile, add the strained lemon juice to the tangerine juice. Add the caster (superfine) sugar and stir from time to time until the sugar has dissolved completely. Still-freeze until slushy.

Whip the cream with the iced water until it forms soft peaks.

Tip the partially-frozen ice into a chilled bowl and beat it thoroughly. Add the egg mousse and beat them lightly together. Finally, add the cream and beat it in lightly. Return the mixture to the freezer trays and still-freeze, whisking once more during freezing.
Note: Approximately 750 g/1 1/2 lb tangerines should give 300 ml/1/2 pint/1 1/4 cups juice.

Lime Sorbet

METRIC/IMPERIAL	AMERICAN
4 limes	4 limes
450 ml/³/4 pint water	2 cups water
225 g/8 oz granulated sugar	1 cup sugar
2 egg whites	2 egg whites
2 tablespoons icing sugar	2 tablespoons confectioners' sugar
green food colouring (optional)	green food coloring (optional)

Finely grate the rind from one of the limes and set it aside. Cut the rind from the remaining limes using a very sharp knife, taking care not to include any of the pith. Put the cut rind in a pan with the water and sugar and slowly heat the mixture until the sugar has dissolved completely. Raise the heat and boil the syrup for 5 minutes, then set it aside to cool.

Squeeze the juice from the limes and combine with the cold syrup. Strain the mixture. Pour into freezer trays and still-freeze until slushy.

Beat the egg whites until foamy, add the icing (confectioners') sugar and continue beating until the meringue holds stiff peaks.

Tip the partially frozen ice into a chilled bowl and beat it thoroughly. Add the meringue and reserved grated peel and whisk them lightly together. Return to the freezer trays and still-freeze, whisking the mixture once more during freezing.

Lemon Ice Cream

METRIC/IMPERIAL	AMERICAN
3 lemons	3 lemons
175 g/6 oz caster sugar	³/4 cup superfine sugar
450 ml/³/4 pint double cream	2 cups heavy cream
3 tablespoons iced water	3 tablespoons iced water

Finely grate the rind from 2 of the lemons and reserve it. Squeeze the juice from the fruit and combine it with the sugar. Stir from time to time until the sugar has dissolved completely.

Whip the cream with the iced water until it forms soft peaks. Beat in the sweetened lemon juice and rind. Pour into freezer trays and still-freeze, whisking the mixture once during freezing, if necessary.

Variation:
Substitute limes for lemons.

From left: GRAPEFRUIT AND MINT SORBET *(page 26)*,
TANGERINE ICE CREAM *(page 27)*, LEMON ICE CREAM,
LIME SORBET

Peach Ice Cream

METRIC/IMPERIAL	AMERICAN
750 g/1 ½ lb ripe peaches	1 ½ lb ripe peaches
juice of 1 orange	juice of 1 orange
4 egg yolks	4 egg yolks
100 g/4 oz icing sugar	1 cup confectioners' sugar
250 ml/8 fl oz double cream	1 cup heavy cream
2 tablespoons iced water	2 tablespoons iced water

Peel and stone (pit) the peaches. Purée the flesh in a blender or press it through a sieve and mix the pulp with the orange juice. Chill.

Beat the egg yolks lightly with the icing (confectioners') sugar. Set the bowl over a pan of just simmering water and continue beating. When the mixture is lukewarm, take the bowl off the heat and continue beating until the mixture is cool and has tripled its original volume. Chill.

Whip the cream with the iced water until it forms soft peaks. Combine the peach purée with the egg mousse and whipped cream and beat them lightly together. Pour into freezer trays and still-freeze, whisking the mixture once during freezing.

Variations:
When fresh peaches are out of season, substitute canned peaches. Drain the fruit well and add the juice of 1 lemon.

Pear Ice Cream

METRIC/IMPERIAL	AMERICAN
750 g/1 ½ lb ripe pears	1 ½ lb ripe pears
juice of 1 lemon	juice of 1 lemon
225 g/8 oz granulated sugar	1 cup sugar
2 tablespoons Kirsch (optional)	2 tablespoons Kirsch (optional)
300 ml/½ pint double cream	1 ¼ cups heavy cream
2 tablespoons iced water	2 tablespoons iced water

Peel, core and roughly chop the pears. Process the fruit in a blender with the lemon juice, sugar and Kirsch. Chill the sweetened pear purée for about 2 hours.

Whip the cream with the iced water until it forms soft peaks. Combine the chilled purée and whipped cream and beat them lightly together. Pour into freezer trays and still-freeze, whisking the mixture once or twice during freezing.

Gooseberry Ice Cream

METRIC/IMPERIAL	AMERICAN
450 g/1 lb gooseberries	*3 ½ cups gooseberries*
100 g/4 oz granulated sugar	*½ cup sugar*
300 ml/½ pint water	*1 ¼ cups water*
4 egg yolks	*4 egg yolks*
100 g/4 oz icing sugar	*1 cup confectioners' sugar*
300 ml/½ pint double cream	*1 ¼ cups heavy cream*
2 tablespoons iced water	*2 tablespoons iced water*
green food colouring (optional)	*green food coloring (optional)*

Wash the gooseberries and put them in a pan with the granulated sugar and water and bring slowly to the boil. Cover and simmer until tender, about 5 minutes depending on the ripeness of the fruit; cool. Purée the fruit by processing in a blender and straining it or passing through a sieve. Chill the purée.

Beat the egg yolks lightly with the icing (confectioners') sugar. Set the bowl over a pan of just simmering water and continue beating. When the mixture is lukewarm, take the bowl off the heat and continue beating until the mixture has tripled its original volume; chill.

Whip the cream with the iced water until it forms soft peaks. Combine the gooseberry purée, egg mousse and whipped cream and beat them lightly together. Add a few drops of green food colouring to make the mixture a pale green, if necessary.

Pour the mixture into freezer trays and still-freeze, whisking the mixture once during freezing, if necessary.

Plum Ice Cream

METRIC/IMPERIAL	AMERICAN
450 g/1 lb plums	1 lb plums
100 g/4 oz granulated sugar	½ cup sugar
150 ml/¼ pint water	⅔ cup water
250 ml/8 fl oz double cream	1 cup heavy cream
2 tablespoons iced water	2 tablespoons iced water
food colouring (optional)	food coloring (optional)

Wash and stone (pit) the plums. Put them in a pan with the sugar and water and bring slowly to the boil. Cover and simmer until tender, about 5 minutes depending on the ripeness of the fruit. Purée the fruit by pressing through a sieve or processing quickly in a blender then straining; chill.

Whip the cream with the iced water until it forms soft peaks. Combine the chilled purée with the whipped cream and beat lightly together. Add a few drops of appropriate food colouring, if necessary. Pour the mixture into freezer trays and still-freeze, whisking the mixture once or twice during freezing.

Cherry Ice Cream

METRIC/IMPERIAL	AMERICAN
1 kg/2 lb cherries	2 lb cherries
juice of 1 lemon	juice of 1 lemon
juice of 1 orange	juice of 1 orange
350 g/12 oz granulated sugar	1½ cups sugar
250 ml/8 fl oz double cream	1 cup heavy cream
2 tablespoons iced water	2 tablespoons iced water

Wash and stone (pit) the cherries. Press through a sieve or process in a blender and strain the purée. Add the lemon and orange juice and the sugar and stir from time to time until the sugar has dissolved completely. Chill for about 2 hours.

Whip the cream with the iced water until it forms soft peaks. Combine the cherry purée with the whipped cream and beat them lightly together. Pour into freezer trays and still-freeze, whisking the mixture once or twice during freezing.

From top left: PEACH *(page 30),* GOOSEBERRY *(page 31)* and PLUM ICE CREAMS. *From top right:* CHERRY, PEAR *(page 30)* and APPLE AND CINNAMON *(page 34)* ICE CREAMS

Iced Raspberry Soufflé

METRIC/IMPERIAL	AMERICAN
350 g/12 oz raspberries	2½ cups raspberries
175 g/6 oz granulated sugar	¾ cup sugar
2 egg whites	2 egg whites
50 g/2 oz icing sugar	½ cup confectioners' sugar
300 ml/½ pint double cream	1¼ cups heavy cream
2 tablespoons iced water	2 tablespoons iced water

Purée the raspberries through a fine sieve or process quickly in a blender and strain the purée. Add the granulated sugar and refrigerate the purée for about 2 hours.

Whisk the egg whites until foamy, add the icing (confectioners') sugar and continue beating until the meringue holds stiff peaks. Whip the cream with the iced water until it forms soft peaks. Combine the chilled raspberry purée, meringue and whipped cream and beat them lightly together. Freeze in one large dish or individual ramekins or glasses, without further beating.

Apple and Cinnamon Ice Cream

METRIC/IMPERIAL	AMERICAN
450 g/1 lb cooking apples	1 lb cooking apples
juice of 1 lemon	juice of 1 lemon
2 teaspoons ground cinnamon	2 teaspoons ground cinnamon
150 ml/¼ pint water	⅔ cup water
175 g/6 oz soft brown sugar	1 cup soft brown sugar
300 ml/½ pint double cream	1¼ cups heavy cream
2 tablespoons iced water	2 tablespoons iced water

Peel, core and roughly chop the apples. Put in a pan with the lemon, cinnamon, water and sugar. Bring slowly to the boil, cover and simmer gently until the apples are soft, about 10 minutes. Cool and purée the mixture in a blender or press through a sieve; chill.

Whip the cream with the iced water until it forms soft peaks. Combine the apple purée with the whipped cream and beat them lightly together. Pour into freezer trays and still-freeze, whisking the mixture once or twice during freezing.

Variation:
Omit the cinnamon and flavour the mixture with 2 to 4 tablespoons of Calvados or brandy.

Raspberry Ice Cream

METRIC/IMPERIAL
350 g/12 oz raspberries, fresh or
* frozen*
juice of 1 orange
juice of 1 lemon
175 g/6 oz granulated sugar
450 ml/³/4 pint double cream
3 tablespoons iced water

AMERICAN
2¹/2 cups raspberries, fresh or
* frozen*
juice of 1 orange
juice of 1 lemon
³/4 cup sugar
2 cups heavy cream
3 tablespoons iced water

Rub the raspberries through a fine sieve to remove the seeds or
process quickly in a blender and strain the purée.

Mix the raspberry purée with the orange and lemon juices and
sugar. Chill the mixture in the refrigerator for about 2 hours.

Whip the cream with the iced water until it forms soft peaks.
Combine the raspberry purée with the whipped cream and beat them
lightly together. Pour into freezer trays and still-freeze, beating the
mixture once or twice during freezing.

Raspberry Sorbet

METRIC/IMPERIAL
450 g/1 lb raspberries
juice of 2 oranges
225 g/8 oz granulated sugar
2 tablespoons Kirsch (optional)
2 egg whites
2 tablespoons icing sugar

AMERICAN
3¹/4 cups raspberries
juice of 2 oranges
1 cup sugar
2 tablespoons Kirsch (optional)
2 egg whites
2 tablespoons confectioners' sugar

Rub the raspberries through a fine sieve to remove the seeds, or
process quickly in a blender and strain the purée.

Mix the raspberry purée with the orange juice, granulated sugar
and Kirsch, if using. Refrigerate the purée for at least an hour. Pour
into freezer trays and still-freeze until slushy.

Beat the egg whites until foamy, add the icing (confectioners')
sugar, and continue beating until the meringue holds stiff peaks. Tip
the partially frozen ice into a chilled bowl and beat thoroughly. Add
the meringue and beat them lightly together. Return to the freezer
trays and still-freeze, beating the mixture once more during freezing.

STORECUPBOARD FLAVOURS

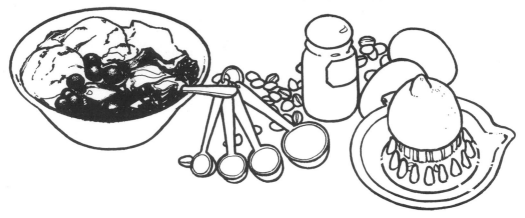

Coffee Parfait

Parfaits are frozen without whisking, so freeze this dessert in pretty glasses or bowls.

METRIC/IMPERIAL	AMERICAN
225 g/8 oz granulated sugar	1 cup sugar
150 ml/¼ pint water	⅔ cup water
4 egg yolks	4 egg yolks
5 tablespoons very strong coffee	5 tablespoons very strong coffee
250 ml/8 fl oz double cream	1 cup heavy cream
2 tablespoons iced water	2 tablespoons iced water
2 egg whites	2 egg whites
2 tablespoons icing sugar	2 tablespoons confectioners' sugar

Put the granulated sugar and water in a small heavy based pan and heat slowly until the sugar has dissolved completely. Raise the heat and boil the syrup, without stirring, until it just begins to turn yellow at the edges. Take the pan off the heat immediately and set aside to cool for a minute or two.

Beat the egg yolks in a large bowl, and still beating, slowly add the hot syrup and coffee. When it is all incorporated continue beating until the egg mousse is cold and has tripled its original volume. Chill.

Whip the cream with the iced water until it forms soft peaks. Whisk the egg whites until foamy, add the icing (confectioners') sugar and continue beating until the meringue holds stiff peaks.

Combine the coffee mousse with the whipped cream and meringue and beat lightly together. Spoon the mixture into individual serving dishes or one large bowl. Still-freeze, without stirring.

From front left: COFFEE ICE CREAM *(page 38)*, RICH COFFEE ICE CREAM *(page 38)*, CAPPUCINO ICE CREAM *(page 39)* AND COFFEE PARFAIT

Coffee Ice Cream

METRIC/IMPERIAL
750 ml/1 ¼ pints milk
2 tablespoons instant coffee
6 egg yolks
225 g/8 oz caster sugar
pinch of salt

AMERICAN
3 cups milk
2 tablespoons instant coffee
6 egg yolks
1 cup superfine sugar
pinch of salt

Warm the milk in a pan and add the coffee. Stir until is has dissolved, then remove the pan from the heat and set aside.

Beat the egg yolks, sugar and salt together until the mixture is very pale and the whisk leaves a trail. Slowly add the warm milk, whisking all the time. Return the mixture to the pan and cook over a very low heat, stirring constantly, until the custard is thick enough to coat the back of a wooden spoon. Set the custard aside and stir it occasionally while it cools.

Pour into freezer trays and still-freeze, whisking the mixture once or twice during freezing.

Rich Coffee Ice Cream

METRIC/IMPERIAL
150 ml/¼ pint single cream
150 ml/¼ pint strong coffee, made
 from coffee beans
4 egg yolks
100 g/4 oz caster sugar
300 ml/½ pint double cream
2 tablespoons iced water

AMERICAN
⅔ cup light cream
⅔ cup strong coffee, made from
 coffee beans
4 egg yolks
½ cup superfine sugar
1 ¼ cups heavy cream
2 tablespoons iced water

Combine the single (light) cream and coffee in a pan and warm the mixture. Remove from the heat and set aside.

Beat the egg yolks and sugar together until the mixture is very pale and the whisk leaves a trail. Slowly add the warm coffee cream, whisking all the time. Return the mixture to the pan and cook over a very low heat, stirring constantly, until the custard is thick enough to coat the back of a wooden spoon. Set the custard aside and stir it occasionally while it cools, then chill it in the refrigerator.

Whip the double (heavy) cream with the iced water until it forms soft peaks. Combine the whipped cream with the coffee custard and beat them lightly together. Pour into freezer trays and still-freeze, whisking the mixture once or twice during freezing.

Cappucino Ice Cream

METRIC/IMPERIAL	AMERICAN
750 ml/1 ¼ pints milk	3 cups milk
100 g/4 oz plain chocolate	4 squares semi-sweet chocolate
1 tablespoon instant coffee	1 tablespoon instant coffee
6 egg yolks	6 egg yolks
175 g/6 oz caster sugar	¾ cup superfine sugar
pinch of salt	pinch of salt

Slowly heat the milk with the chocolate broken into small pieces; stir until the chocolate has melted completely. Remove from the heat, add the coffee, and stir until it has dissolved. Set aside.

Beat the egg yolks, sugar and salt together until the mixture is very pale and the whisk leaves a trail. Slowly add the strained, flavoured milk, whisking all the time. Return the mixture to the pan and cook over a very low heat, stirring constantly, until the custard is thick enough to coat the back of a wooden spoon. Set the custard aside and stir it occasionally as it cools. Pour into freezer trays and still-freeze, whisking the mixture once or twice during freezing.

Caramel Ice Cream

METRIC/IMPERIAL	AMERICAN
100 g/4 oz granulated sugar	½ cup sugar
750 ml/1 ¼ pints milk	3 cups milk
6 egg yolks	6 egg yolks
100 g/4 oz caster sugar	½ cup superfine sugar
pinch of salt	pinch of salt

Put the granulated sugar in a large, heavy-based pan and heat it slowly until it has caramelized to a deep golden brown. Take the pan off the heat and immediately add the cold milk; take care when adding the milk as the caramel will bubble up fiercely. Stir until the caramel has dissolved, then set aside.

Beat the egg yolks, caster (superfine) sugar and salt together until the mixture is very pale and the whisk leaves a trail. Slowly add the warm caramel milk, whisking all the time. Return the mixture to the pan and cook carefully over a very low heat, stirring constantly, until the custard is thick enough to coat the back of a wooden spoon. Set the custard aside and stir it occasionally as it cools.

Pour into freezer trays and still-freeze, whisking the mixture once or twice during freezing.

Variation:
Chopped, toasted nuts (hazelnuts, walnuts, pecans or Brazil nuts) can be added to the partially frozen mixture, after whisking.

Tea Ice Cream

METRIC/IMPERIAL	AMERICAN
4 egg yolks	*4 egg yolks*
100 g/4 oz caster sugar	*½ cup superfine sugar*
pinch of salt	*pinch of salt*
150 ml/¼ pint milk	*⅔ cup milk*
150 ml/¼ pint strong tea	*⅔ cup strong tea*
300 ml/½ pint double cream	*1¼ cups heavy cream*
2 tablespoons iced water	*2 tablespoons iced water*

Beat the egg yolks, sugar and salt together until the mixture is very pale and the whisk leaves a trail. Slowly add the milk and tea, whisking all the time. Cook the mixture over a very low heat, stirring constantly, until the custard is thick enough to coat the back of a wooden spoon. Set the custard aside and stir it occasionally as it cools. Chill.

Whip the cream with the iced water until it forms soft peaks. Combine the whipped cream with the chilled custard and beat them lightly together. Pour into freezer trays and still-freeze, whisking the mixture once or twice during freezing.

Butterscotch Ice Cream

METRIC/IMPERIAL	AMERICAN
50 g/2 oz butter	*¼ cup butter*
175 g/6 oz soft brown sugar	*1 cup soft brown sugar*
450 ml/¾ pint hot milk	*2 cups hot milk*
4 egg yolks	*4 egg yolks*
150 ml/¼ pint double cream	*⅔ cup heavy cream*
1 tablespoon iced water	*1 tablespoon iced water*

Melt the butter in a pan and add the sugar. Cook the mixture on a low heat until the sugar just begins to caramelize. Add the milk and stir until the butterscotch has dissolved completely. Set aside to cool slightly.

Beat the egg yolks thoroughly, and still beating, slowly add the hot milk. Strain the mixture and return it to the pan. Cook carefully over a low heat, stirring constantly, until the custard is thick enough to coat the back of a wooden spoon. Set the custard aside and stir it occasionally as it cools. Chill.

Whip the cream with the iced water until it forms soft peaks. Combine the chilled custard and whipped cream and beat them lightly together. Pour into freezer trays and still-freeze, whisking the mixture once or twice during freezing.

From front left: RASPBERRY ICE CREAM *(page 35),*
ICED RASPBERRY SOUFFLÉ *(page 34)* and
RASPBERRY SORBET *(page 35)*

Chocolate and Orange Ice Cream

METRIC/IMPERIAL	AMERICAN
175 ml/6 fl oz sweetened condensed milk	¾ cup sweetened condensed milk
100 g/4 oz plain chocolate	4 squares semi-sweet chocolate
1 teaspoon vanilla essence	1 teaspoon vanilla extract
300 ml/½ pint double cream	1¼ cups heavy cream
2 tablespoons iced water	2 tablespoons iced water
100 g/4 oz chocolate covered candied orange peel, chopped	⅔ cup chopped chocolate covered candied orange peel
4 tablespoons orange liqueur	¼ cup orange liqueur

Heat the condensed milk with the chocolate broken in small pieces; stir until the chocolate has melted. Cool and chill the mixture. Add the vanilla and whisk the mixture thoroughly.

Whisk the cream with the iced water until it forms soft peaks. Combine the whipped cream with the chocolate mixture and the remaining ingredients and beat them lightly together. Pour into freezer trays and still-freeze until firm.

Chocolate and Burnt Almond Ice Cream

METRIC/IMPERIAL	AMERICAN
1 litre/1¾ pint Chocolate Ice Cream	4¼ cups Chocolate Ice Cream
100 g/4 oz blanched, slivered almonds	1 cup blanched, slivered almonds
4 tablespoons brandy	¼ cup brandy

Make Chocolate Ice Cream (see page 44), and freeze the mixture until it is half-frozen. Whisk it thoroughly. Alternatively, soften already made ice cream by transferring it to the refrigerator for 30 minutes or more.

Spread the slivered almonds on a baking sheet and toast them in a preheated moderate oven (160°C/325°F, Gas Mark 3) for about 12 minutes, or until they are well browned. Cool and crush the burnt almonds.

Combine the almonds and brandy with the partially frozen or softened ice cream. Mix well to distribute the nuts evenly throughout the mixture. Still-freeze until firm.
Makes about 1.2 litres/2 pints/5 cups

Almond Macaroon Ice Cream

Use homemade ratafias, page 87, or crisp, bought macaroons for this recipe.

METRIC/IMPERIAL	AMERICAN
4 egg yolks	4 egg yolks
100 g/4 oz caster sugar	1/2 cup sugar
300 ml/1/2 pint milk	1 1/4 cups milk
1/2 teaspoon almond essence	1/2 teaspoon almond extract
250 ml/8 fl oz double cream	1 cup heavy cream
2 tablespoons iced water	2 tablespoons iced water
50 g/2 oz ratafias, crushed	2 oz ratafias, crushed

Beat the egg yolks and sugar together until the mixture is very pale and the whisk leaves a trail. Slowly add the milk, whisking all the time. Pour the mixture into a saucepan.

Cook the mixture over a low heat, stirring constantly, until the custard is thick enough to coat the back of a wooden spoon. Set it aside to cool, stirring occasionally. Add the almond essence (extract), mix well, and chill the custard.

Whip the cream with the iced water until it forms soft peaks. Combine the chilled custard with the whipped cream and crushed ratafias and beat lightly together. Pour into freezing trays and still-freeze, whisking the mixture once or twice during freezing.

Chocolate Ice Cream

Use a good plain (semi-sweet) chocolate for this tasty ice cream.

METRIC/IMPERIAL	AMERICAN
6 egg yolks	6 egg yolks
100 g/4 oz caster sugar	½ cup superfine sugar
600 ml/1 pint milk	2½ cups milk
225 g/8 oz plain chocolate	8 squares semi-sweet chocolate
1 teaspoon vanilla essence	1 teaspoon vanilla extract

Beat the egg yolks and sugar together until the mixture is very pale and the whisk leaves a trail. Slowly add the milk, whisking all the time. Pour the mixture into a pan.

Cook over a very low heat, stirring constantly, until the custard is thick enough to coat the back of a wooden spoon. Remove from the heat and cool the custard for 5 minutes at room temperature.

Grate the chocolate into the warm custard and stir until it has melted completely, then add the vanilla. Pour into freezer trays and still–freeze, whisking the mixture once or twice during freezing.

Chocolate Velvet Ice Cream

METRIC/IMPERIAL	AMERICAN
175 ml/6 fl oz sweetened condensed milk	¾ cup sweetened condensed milk
100 g/4 oz plain chocolate	4 squares semi-sweet chocolate
1 teaspoon vanilla essence	1 teaspoon vanilla extract
350 ml/12 fl oz double cream	1½ cups heavy cream
2 tablespoons iced water	2 tablespoons iced water

Heat the condensed milk with the chocolate broken in small pieces; stir until the chocolate has melted. Cool and chill the mixture. Add the vanilla and whisk the chocolate mixture thoroughly.

Whisk the cream with the iced water until it forms soft peaks. Combine the whipped cream with the chocolate mixture and whisk them lightly together. Pour into freezer trays and still–freeze until firm. This can be frozen without whisking.

From left: CHOCOLATE ICE CREAM, CHOCOLATE MINT ICE CREAM *(page 46)* WITH CHOCOLATE SAUCE *(page 78)*, CHOCOLATE AND BURNT ALMOND ICE CREAM *(page 43)*, CHOCOLATE AND ORANGE ICE CREAM *(page 42)*, AND CHOCOLATE VELVET ICE CREAM

Chocolate Mint Ice Cream

METRIC/IMPERIAL	AMERICAN
4 egg yolks	4 egg yolks
175 g/6 oz caster sugar	¾ cup superfine sugar
300 ml/½ pint milk	1¼ cups milk
100 g/4 oz plain chocolate	4 squares semi-sweet chocolate
2 tablespoons crème de menthe or brandy	2 tablespoons crème de menthe or brandy
50 g/2 oz chocolate mint crisps, grated	⅓ cup grated chocolate mint crisps
250 ml/8 fl oz double cream	1 cup heavy cream
2 tablespoons iced water	2 tablespoons iced water

Beat the egg yolks and sugar together until the mixture is very pale and the whisk leaves a trail. Slowly add the milk, whisking all the time. Cook the mixture over a low heat, stirring constantly, until the custard is thick enough to coat the back of a wooden spoon. Remove from the heat and cool the custard for 5 minutes at room temperature.

Grate the chocolate into the warm custard and stir until it has melted completely; chill. Stir the liqueur and grated mint crisps into the chilled chocolate custard.

Whip the cream with the iced water until it forms soft peaks. Combine the whipped cream with the chocolate custard and beat them lightly together. Pour into freezer trays and still-freeze, whisking the mixture once or twice during freezing.

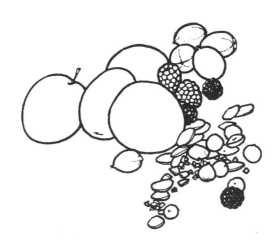

CHILDREN'S ICES

Banana Ice Cream

METRIC/IMPERIAL	AMERICAN
175 ml/6 fl oz sweetened condensed milk	3/4 cup sweetened condensed milk
250 ml/8 fl oz double cream	1 cup heavy cream
5 bananas	5 bananas
juice of 1 lemon	juice of 1 lemon
2 tablespoons caster sugar	2 tablespoons superfine sugar

Mix the condensed milk and cream in a large bowl and chill in the refrigerator for 30 minutes.

Peel and purée the bananas by processing them in a blender or pressing them through a nylon sieve. Add the lemon juice and sugar.

Whisk the cream mixture until it forms stiff peaks. Add the banana purée and whip them lightly together. Pour into freezing trays and still-freeze until firm. It is not necessary to whisk the mixture during freezing.

Variation:
If liked, flavour the mixture with 2 tablespoons dark rum.

Chocolate Chip Ice Cream

METRIC/IMPERIAL
1 litre/1 ¾ pints Vanilla Ice Cream
100 g/4 oz plain chocolate, finely
 grated

AMERICAN
4 ¼ cups Vanilla Ice Cream
4 squares semi-sweet chocolate,
 finely grated

Make the Vanilla Ice Cream (see pages 11 to 14), and still-freeze the mixture until half-frozen. Whisk it thoroughly. Alternatively, soften already made ice cream by transferring it to the refrigerator for 30 minutes or more.

Combine the partially frozen or softened ice cream with the grated chocolate. Mix just enough to distribute the chocolate evenly throughout the mixture. Still-freeze until firm.

Peppermint Rock Ice Cream

METRIC/IMPERIAL
300 ml/½ pint milk
100 g/4 oz peppermint rock,
 crushed
4 egg yolks
300 ml/½ pint double cream
2 tablespoons iced water
red food colouring (optional)

AMERICAN
1 ¼ cups milk
¼ lb peppermint stick candy,
 crushed
4 egg yolks
1 ¼ cups heavy cream
2 tablespoons iced water
red food coloring (optional)

Slowly heat together the milk and crushed rock (candy), stirring until it has dissolved completely. Remove from the heat and set aside.

Whisk the egg yolks in a bowl, and still whisking, slowly add the peppermint milk. Return the mixture to the pan and cook over a very low heat, stirring constantly, until the custard is thick enough to coat the back of a wooden spoon. Set the custard aside and stir occasionally while it cools.

Whip the cream with the iced water until it forms soft peaks. Fold the whipped cream into the cold custard. Add a few drops of red food colouring, if liked, to make the ice a bright candy pink. Pour into freezer trays and still-freeze, whisking the mixture once or twice during freezing.

CHOCOLATE CHIP ICE CREAM, BANANA ICE CREAM
(page 47), WITH STRAWBERRY SAUCE *(page 79)* and
PEPPERMINT ROCK ICE CREAM

Peach Melba Yogurt Ice

METRIC/IMPERIAL
2 egg whites
2 tablespoons icing sugar
600 ml/1 pint peach melba yogurt

AMERICAN
2 egg whites
2 tablespoons confectioners' sugar
2 ½ cups peach melba yogurt

Whisk the egg whites until foamy, add the icing (confectioners') sugar and continue whisking until the meringue holds stiff peaks. Add the yogurt and beat the mixture lightly. Pour into freezer trays and still-freeze, whisking the mixture once or twice during freezing.

Raspberry Yogurt Ice

METRIC/IMPERIAL
225 g/8 oz raspberries
100 g/4 oz granulated sugar
450 ml/³/4 pint natural yogurt
2 egg whites
2 tablespoons icing sugar

AMERICAN
1 ²/3 cups raspberries
½ cup sugar
2 cups natural yogurt
2 egg whites
2 tablespoons confectioners' sugar

Rub the raspberries through a sieve to remove the seeds, or process them lightly in a blender and strain the purée. Add the granulated sugar and yogurt, stir well, and refrigerate the mixture for about 30 minutes.

Whisk the egg whites until foamy, add the icing (confectioners') sugar, and continue whisking until the meringue holds stiff peaks. Combine the chilled raspberry yogurt with the meringue and beat them lightly together. Pour into freezer trays and still-freeze, whisking the mixture once or twice during freezing.

Variation:
Other fruits may be used – strawberry, peach, pineapple or banana.

Honey Yogurt Ice

METRIC/IMPERIAL	AMERICAN
600 ml/1 pint plain yogurt	2 1/2 cups unflavored yogurt
4 tablespoons clear honey	1/4 cup clear honey
2 egg whites	2 egg whites
2 tablespoons icing sugar	2 tablespoons confectioners' sugar

Combine the yogurt and honey and chill for about 30 minutes.

Whisk the egg whites until foamy, add the sugar and continue beating until the meringue holds stiff peaks.

Combine the yogurt mixture with the meringue and beat lightly together. Pour into freezer trays and still-freeze, whisking the mixture once or twice during freezing.

Greengage Yogurt Ice Cream

METRIC/IMPERIAL	AMERICAN
350 g/12 oz canned greengages, stoned and drained	3 cups canned greengages, pitted and drained
50 g/2 oz caster sugar	1/4 cup superfine sugar
450 ml/3/4 pint plain yogurt	2 cups unflavored yogurt
150 ml/1/4 pint soured cream	2/3 cup sour cream
2 egg whites	2 egg whites
2 tablespoons icing sugar	2 tablespoons confectioners' sugar

Rub the greengages through a sieve, or process them quickly in a blender and strain the purée. Add the caster (superfine) sugar and stir from time to time until it has dissolved completely.

Combine the sweetened purée with the yogurt and soured (sour) cream and mix them well together.

Whisk the egg whites until foamy, add the icing (confectioners') sugar, and continue beating until the meringue holds stiff peaks.

Combine the greengage mixture with the meringue and beat them lightly together. Pour into freezer trays and still-freeze, whisking the mixture once or twice during freezing.

Orange Ice Lollies (Popsicles)

Frozen ices (popsicles) on sticks are easy to make with fresh or canned fruit juice, sweetened to taste. Orange squash, cordial, or concentrated frozen juice, diluted to taste, work just as well. Use this recipe to make ice lollies with other fruit juices too, pineapple, grapefruit, lime and blackcurrant are good.

Special moulds for making ice lollies (popsicles) are sold in department stores, along with refills of rolled paper sticks which do not splinter.

METRIC/IMPERIAL	AMERICAN
1 teaspoon gelatine	*1 teaspoon unflavored gelatin*
6 tablespoons water	*6 tablespoons water*
300 ml/½ pint orange juice, sweetened to taste	*1¼ cups orange juice, sweetened to taste*

Combine the gelatine and water in a small pan and heat slowly, stirring until the gelatine dissolves.

Mix the dissolved gelatine with the juice, stir well, and pour into moulds.

Freeze until firm. Unmould the lollies and serve immediately, or stack the ices between sheets of greaseproof paper or foil and store in the freezer until needed.
Makes 6

Strawberry Yogurt Lollies

METRIC/IMPERIAL	AMERICAN
1 teaspoon gelatine	*1 teaspoon unflavored gelatin*
150 ml/¼ pint milk	*⅔ cup milk*
250 ml/8 fl oz strawberry yogurt	*1 cup strawberry yogurt*

Combine the gelatine and milk in a small pan and heat slowly stirring until the gelatine dissolves.

Mix the milk and gelatine with the yogurt and pour the mixture into moulds. Freeze until firm. Unmould the lollies and serve immediately, or stack the ices between sheets of greaseproof paper or foil and store in the freezer until needed.
Makes 6

Variation:
Any other flavoured yogurt can be used in place of the strawberry – choose strong flavours such as black cherry or apricot.

ICE LOLLIES (POPSICLES) *From left:* BLACKCURRANT, ORANGE, STRAWBERRY YOGURT, LIME, APRICOT YOGURT AND GRAPEFRUIT

TRAVELLERS' JOYS

Melon and Ginger Ice Cream

METRIC/IMPERIAL
1 melon, about 450 g/1 lb
juice of 1 lemon
175 g/6 oz caster sugar
300 ml/1/2 pint double cream
2 tablespoons iced water
50 g/2 oz crystallized ginger,
  chopped

AMERICAN
1 melon, about 1 lb
juice of 1 lemon
3/4 cup superfine sugar
1 1/4 cups heavy cream
2 tablespoons iced water
1/4 cup chopped preserved
  ginger

Halve the melon, discard the seeds and scoop out the flesh. Purée by pressing it through a sieve or processing it in a blender. Add the lemon juice and sugar, and stir from time to time until the sugar has dissolved completely. Pour into freezer trays and still–freeze the melon purée until slushy.

Whip the cream with the iced water until it forms soft peaks.

Tip the partially frozen ice into a chilled bowl and whisk it thoroughly. Add the whipped cream and chopped ginger and beat them lightly together. Return to the freezer trays and still–freeze, whisking the mixture once more during freezing.

Coconut Ice Cream

Coconut ice cream is extremely popular throughout the Caribbean, Mexico and Brazil.

METRIC/IMPERIAL
600 ml/1 pint milk
175 g/6 oz grated or desiccated
  coconut
4 egg yolks
100 g/4 oz caster sugar
pinch of salt
300 ml/½ pint double cream
2 tablespoons iced water

AMERICAN
2½ cups milk
2 cups grated or shredded coconut
4 egg yolks
½ cup superfine sugar
pinch of salt
1¼ cups heavy cream
2 tablespoons iced water

Boil the milk, stir in the coconut and set the mixture aside to infuse for about 30 minutes. Strain it through a fine sieve, pressing through as much as possible of the coconut flavoured milk.

Beat the egg yolks, sugar and salt together, until the mixture is very pale and the whisk leaves a trail. Slowly add the coconut milk, whisking all the time.

Cook the coconut mixture carefully, stirring constantly, until the custard is thick enough to coat the back of a wooden spoon. Set the custard aside and stir it occasionally as it cools.

Whip the cream with the iced water until it forms soft peaks. Combine the whipped cream with the chilled custard and beat them lightly together. Pour into freezer trays and still-freeze, whisking the mixture once or twice during freezing.

Pineapple Ice Cream

METRIC/IMPERIAL
1 pineapple, about 750 g/1½ lb
225 g/8 oz caster sugar
300 ml/½ pint double cream
2 tablespoons iced water

AMERICAN
1 pineapple, about 1½ lb
1 cup superfine sugar
1¼ cups heavy cream
2 tablespoons iced water

Chop the top off the pineapple and cut the flesh in thick slices. Trim away the skin and 'eyes' and remove the hard core. Roughly chop the flesh and process it lightly in a blender. Strain the purée, add the sugar and chill the mixture for at least an hour.

Whip the cream with the iced water until it forms soft peaks. Combine the pineapple purée with the whipped cream and beat them lightly together. Pour into freezer trays and still-freeze, whisking the mixture once or twice during freezing.

Pistachio Kulfi

Pistachios and cardamom give a fresh and unusual flavour to this delicate Indian ice which is traditionally frozen in individual moulds. Divide the mixture between cream, yogurt cartons, or small tumblers and freeze; turn out the ices just before serving.

METRIC/IMPERIAL	AMERICAN
1.5 litres/2½ pints milk	6¼ cups milk
4 tablespoons granulated sugar	¼ cup sugar
2 tablespoons finely chopped pistachio kernels	2 tablespoons finely chopped pistachio kernels
1 teaspoon ground cardamom	1 teaspoon ground cardamom

Put the milk in a large, heavy based pan or casserole and bring it almost to the boil. Adjust the heat so that the milk keeps bubbling but does not rise and boil over. Keep the milk at this temperature, stirring frequently, until it has reduced to about 600 ml/1 pint/2½ cups. Remove from the heat. Boiling down the milk will take about 1 hour.

Add the sugar, nuts and cardamom, and stir until the sugar has dissolved completely. Set the mixture aside to cool.

Divide the mixture between six moulds and still-freeze stirring each ice two or three times during freezing.

Makes 6

From front: MELON SHERBET *(page 58)*, PISTACHIO KULFIS, MELON AND GINGER ICE CREAM *(page 54)*

Papaya Ice Cream

There are papayas as big as pumpkins in the street markets of
tropical countries, but exported fruit is usually about the size of an
avocado.

METRIC/IMPERIAL	AMERICAN
450 g/1 lb papayas	*1 lb papayas*
100 g/4 oz granulated sugar	*½ cup granulated sugar*
juice of 2 limes	*juice of 2 limes*
450 ml/¾ pint double cream	*2 cups heavy cream*
3 tablespoons iced water	*3 tablespoons iced water*

Cut the papayas in halves and scoop out the black seeds. Spoon out
the flesh and press it through a sieve, or process it lightly in a blender
and strain the purée. Mix the purée with the sugar and lime juice and
refrigerate the mixture for at least an hour.

Whip the cream with the iced water until it forms soft peaks.
Combine the whipped cream with the papaya purée and beat lightly
together. Pour into freezer trays and still-freeze, whisking the
mixture once or twice during freezing.

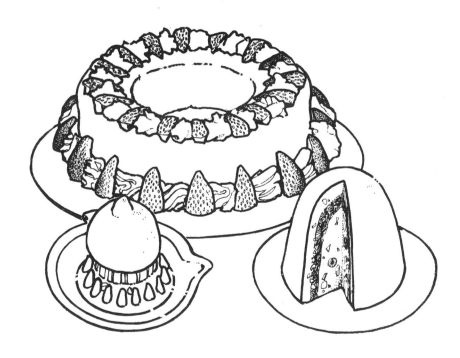

Mango Ice Cream

METRIC/IMPERIAL	AMERICAN
4 egg yolks	4 egg yolks
100 g/4 oz icing sugar	1 cup confectioners' sugar
450 g/1 lb mango	1 lb mango
250 ml/8 fl oz double cream	1 cup heavy cream
2 tablespoons iced water	2 tablespoons iced water

Beat the egg yolks lightly with the icing (confectioners') sugar. Set the bowl over a pan of just simmering water and continue beating. When the mixture is lukewarm, take the bowl off the heat and continue beating until it is cool and has tripled its original volume. Chill the egg mousse.

Peel the mango and remove the stone. Rub the flesh through a sieve, or process it lightly in a blender and strain the purée.

Whip the cream with the iced water until it forms soft peaks. Combine the egg mousse, mango purée and whipped cream and beat them lightly together. Pour into freezer trays and still-freeze, whisking the mixture once or twice during freezing.

Melon Sherbet

METRIC/IMPERIAL	AMERICAN
175 g/6 oz granulated sugar	¾ cup sugar
300 ml/½ pint water	1¼ cups water
1 melon, about 750 g/1½ lb	1 melon, about 1½ lb
juice of 1 orange	juice of 1 orange
juice of 1 lemon	juice of 1 lemon

Put the sugar in a small pan with the water and heat slowly until the sugar has dissolved completely. Raise the heat and boil the syrup for 5 minutes, then set aside to cool.

Halve the melon, discard the seeds, and scoop out the flesh. Purée the flesh by pressing it through a sieve or processing it lightly in a blender. Combine the melon purée, cold syrup, orange and lemon juice. Pour into freezer trays and still-freeze, whisking the mixture once or twice during freezing.

Guava Ice Cream

Fresh, ripe guavas have a strong scent and flavour. To substitute canned guava in this recipe, purée 225 g/8 oz/½ lb of drained flesh with the juice of a fresh lime or lemon.

METRIC/IMPERIAL	AMERICAN
450 g/1 lb guavas	1 lb guavas
100 g/4 oz granulated sugar	½ cup sugar
4 tablespoons water	¼ cup water
4 egg yolks	4 egg yolks
100 g/4 oz caster sugar	½ cup superfine sugar
450 ml/¾ pint milk	2 cups milk

Peel the guavas and remove the seeds. Roughly chop the flesh and put it in a pan with the granulated sugar and water. Heat slowly until the sugar has dissolved completely, then raise the heat and simmer the mixture until the guavas are tender, about 5 minutes. Press the fruit and syrup through a sieve, or process it lightly in a blender and strain the purée. Set aside to cool.

Beat the egg yolks and sugar together until the mixture is very pale and the whisk leaves a trail. Slowly add the milk, whisking all the time. Cook the custard over a low heat, stirring constantly, until it is thick enough to coat the back of a wooden spoon. Set the custard aside and stir it occasionally as it cools.

Combine the cold guava purée with the custard and beat them lightly together. Pour into freezer trays and still-freeze, whisking the mixture once or twice during freezing.

From left: GUAVA, PINEAPPLE (page 55), PAPAYA (page 59), AND COCONUT ICE CREAMS (page 55), KIWI FRUIT SORBET (page 62) AND MANGO ICE CREAM (page 59)

Kiwi Fruit Sorbet

METRIC/IMPERIAL	AMERICAN
750 g/1 ½ lb kiwi fruit	*1 ½ lb kiwi fruit*
juice of 2 limes	*juice of 2 limes*
225 g/8 oz granulated sugar	*1 cup sugar*
2 egg whites	*2 egg whites*
2 tablespoons icing sugar	*2 tablespoons confectioners' sugar*

Peel the kiwi fruit and press the flesh through a fine sieve to remove the seeds, or process it lightly in a blender and strain the purée. Mix the purée with the lime juice and granulated sugar and refrigerate the mixture for at least an hour. Pour the mixture into freezer trays and still-freeze until slushy.

Whisk the egg whites until foamy, add the icing (confectioners') sugar and continue whisking until the meringue holds stiff peaks.

Tip the partially-frozen ice into a chilled bowl and beat thoroughly. Add the meringue and beat lightly together. Return to the freezer trays and still-freeze, whisking the mixture once more during freezing.

WINE & SPIRIT ICES

Sauternes Sorbet

The alcohol in sauternes inhibits freezing so the mixture never freezes as hard as usual ice cream and tends to separate during freezing unless beaten at least twice as it firms. The result is so delicious though that it is well worth the trouble.

METRIC/IMPERIAL	AMERICAN
225 g/8 oz granulated sugar	*1 cup sugar*
250 ml/8 fl oz water	*1 cup water*
2 lemons	*2 lemons*
450 ml/³/₄ pint sauternes	*2 cups sauternes*
2 egg whites	*2 egg whites*
2 tablespoons icing sugar	*2 tablespoons confectioners' sugar*

Slowly heat together the sugar and water until the sugar is dissolved completely. Raise the heat and boil for 5 minutes. Take the pan off the heat and add the grated rind of both lemons. Set aside to cool.

Squeeze the juice from the lemons and add it to the cold syrup. Strain the mixture and add it to the wine. Pour into freezer trays and still-freeze until slushy.

Whisk the egg whites until foamy, add the icing (confectioners') sugar and continue whisking until the meringue holds stiff peaks.

Tip the partially-frozen ice into a chilled bowl and whisk it thoroughly. Add the meringue and whisk lightly together. Return to the freezer trays and still-freeze, whisking the mixture two or three times as it firms.

Champagne Ice Cream

The most luxurious of ices, champagne ice cream is a dessert for very special occasions. This recipe can also be made with any sweet white wine.

METRIC/IMPERIAL	AMERICAN
100 g/4 oz granulated sugar	½ cup sugar
150 ml/¼ pint water	⅔ cup water
juice of 1 orange	juice of 1 orange
juice of 1 lemon	juice of 1 lemon
450 ml/¾ pint sweet champagne	2 cups sweet champagne
300 ml/½ pint double cream	1¼ cups heavy cream
2 tablespoons iced water	2 tablespoons iced water

Slowly heat together the sugar and water until the sugar is dissolved completely. Raise the heat and boil the syrup for 5 minutes. Remove the pan from the heat and set it aside to cool.

Combine the strained fruit juice with the cold syrup and champagne. Pour into freezer trays and still-freeze until slushy.

Whip the cream with the iced water until it forms soft peaks.

Tip the partially-frozen ice into a chilled bowl and beat it thoroughly. Add the whipped cream and beat lightly together. Return to the freezer trays and still-freeze, whisking the mixture twice more during freezing.

From left: CHAMPAGNE ICE CREAM, SAUTERNES SORBET *(page 63)* and GRAPE SHERBERT *(page 66)*

Grape Sherbet

METRIC/IMPERIAL
1 kg/2 lb grapes
juice of 2 lemons
225 g/8 oz caster sugar
2 tablespoons Marsala wine

AMERICAN
2 lb grapes
juice of 2 lemons
1 cup superfine sugar
2 tablespoons Marsala wine

Wash the grapes and extract the juice by processing them lightly in a blender or pressing through a sieve.

Combine the strained grape juice with the lemon juice, sugar and Marsala, and stir the mixture until the sugar has dissolved completely. Pour into freezer trays and still-freeze, whisking the mixture once or twice during freezing.

Benedictine Ice Cream

METRIC/IMPERIAL
175 ml/6 fl oz sweetened condensed
  milk
450 ml/3/4 pint double cream
5 tablespoons Benedictine

AMERICAN
3/4 cup sweetened condensed milk
2 cups heavy cream
1/3 cup Benedictine

Combine all the ingredients in a large bowl and chill in the refrigerator for about 30 minutes. Whisk the mixture until it forms stiff peaks. Spoon into freezer trays and still-freeze until firm.

Iced Zabaglione

METRIC/IMPERIAL	AMERICAN
4 egg yolks	*4 egg yolks*
100 g/4 oz caster sugar	*1/2 cup superfine sugar*
150 ml/1/4 pint Marsala	*2/3 cup Marsala*
300 ml/1/2 pint double cream	*1 1/4 cups heavy cream*
2 tablespoons iced water	*2 tablespoons iced water*

Beat the egg yolks and sugar together until the mixture is pale and the whisk leaves a trail. Slowly add the Marsala, whisking all the time. Set the bowl over a pan of just simmering water and whisk until the mixture is thick and has at least doubled in volume. Take the bowl off the heat and continue whisking until the mixture is cool; chill.

Whip the cream with the iced water until it forms soft peaks. Combine the chilled zabaglione with the whipped cream and beat them lightly together.

Spoon the mixture into individual glasses, ramekins or a 900 ml/1 1/2 pint/3 3/4 cup soufflé dish, prepared in the usual way. Still-freeze until firm.

Liqueur Parfaits

METRIC/IMPERIAL	AMERICAN
225 g/8 oz granulated sugar	1 cup sugar
150 ml/¼ pint water	⅔ cup water
4 egg yolks	4 egg yolks
4 tablespoons liqueur	¼ cup liqueur
250 ml/8 fl oz double cream	1 cup heavy cream
2 tablespoons iced water	2 tablespoons iced water
2 egg whites	2 egg whites
2 tablespoons icing sugar	2 tablespoons confectioners' sugar

Put the granulated sugar in a small, heavy based pan with the water and heat slowly until the sugar has dissolved completely. Raise the heat and boil the syrup, without stirring, until it just begins to turn yellow. Take the pan off the heat immediately, and set it aside to cool for a minute or two.

Beat the egg yolks in a large bowl and, still beating, slowly add the hot syrup. When all the syrup is incorporated, continue beating until the egg mousse is cold and has tripled its original volume. Beat in the liqueur and chill the mixture.

Whip the cream with the iced water until it forms soft peaks.

Whisk the egg whites until foamy, add the icing (confectioners') sugar, and continue beating until the meringue holds stiff peaks.

Combine the egg mousse with the whipped cream and meringue and beat lightly together. Spoon the mixture into individual serving dishes or one large bowl. Still-freeze without stirring.

From left: LIQUEUR PARFAITS AND ICED ZABAGLIONE
(page 67) BOTH SERVED WITH VANILLA WAFERS *(page 90)*

PARTY PIECES

Ice Cream Bombes

These moulded ices are a boon to busy cooks. Preparation can be completed days in advance of a dinner or buffet party so that ripening the ices an hour or two before bringing them to table is all that needs to be done on the day.

A bombe is simply two or three flavours of ice cream moulded in layers, usually in a dome shape. Beautiful, lidded copper moulds can be bought for the purpose but they are expensive; and with modern freezers, an ordinary glass or pottery mixing bowl serves very well. A 600 ml/1 pint/2½ cup mould serves 4 to 6 people, and a 1.2 litre/ 2 pint/5 cup mould serves 8 to 12.

The only practical point to bear in mind is the ripening times of the ices you choose. The harder ices should be nearest the outside of the mould, and the softer ices in the centre. In this way, the bombe will ripen evenly and each ice will be just right when it is served. Any of the still-freeze recipes in this book make good bombe centres, and the following basic bombe mousse, when flavoured with a combination of fruit, nuts and liqueurs, is the classic filling.

To Mould a Bombe
Chill the mould or bowl thoroughly in the freezer and 'ripen' the ice cream which is to form the outside layer.

Line the bottom and sides of the mould with the first ice cream spreading it in an even layer right up to the rim. Cover the mould and freeze it until the ice is firm. Ripen the second ice cream.

Remove the mould from the freezer and spread the second ice in an even layer. Cover and freeze until firm. Ripen the third ice cream, or finish with bombe mousse.

Remove the mould from the freezer and fill it with the third ice cream or bombe mousse. Cover and freeze until firm.

Always unmould bombes before ripening the ice cream.

To Unmould a Bombe

Remove the lid or covering from the bombe and invert the mould on to a serving plate.

Wring out a cloth in hot water and wrap it round the mould. It will cool quickly, so repeat this step two or three times.

Hold the mould and plate together and shake them with an up and down motion until the bombe releases its grip on the mould. Carefully lift off the mould. Return the bombe to the freezer for about 10 minutes before smoothing over any blemishes on the shell or tidying up any drips on the plate.

Freeze the shell hard again before wrapping the bombe for storing in the freezer.

Basic Bombe Mousse

This mixture keeps for up to a week in a tightly covered container.

METRIC/IMPERIAL	AMERICAN
100 g/4 oz granulated sugar	*½ cup sugar*
120 ml/4 fl oz water	*½ cup water*
4 egg yolks	*4 egg yolks*

Put the sugar and water in a small pan and heat slowly until the sugar has dissolved completely. Raise the heat and boil the syrup gently for 5 minutes. Set it aside to cool a little.

Beat the egg yolks in a bowl and still beating, slowly add the syrup. Set the bowl over a pan of simmering water and continue beating for about 5 minutes, until the mixture is thick and pale and has tripled in volume.

Stand the bowl in iced water and beat until the mousse is quite cold.

Makes about 600 ml/1 pint/2½ cups

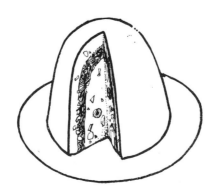

Summer Bombe

Raspberry and vanilla ice cream encase a soft centre of bombe mousse flavoured with cherries soaked in a maraschino flavoured syrup.

METRIC/IMPERIAL
450 ml/¾ pint Raspberry Ice
  Cream (page 35)
300 ml/½ pint Vanilla Ice Cream
  (page 11)
1 egg white, stiffly beaten
2 tablespoons whipped cream
4 tablespoons maraschino cherries,
  roughly chopped
2 tablespoons maraschino syrup
150 ml/¼ pint Basic Bombe
  Mousse (page 71)

AMERICAN
2 cups Raspberry Ice Cream
  (page 35)
1¼ cups Vanilla Ice Cream
  (page 11)
1 egg white, stiffly beaten
2 tablespoons whipped cream
¼ cup maraschino cherries, roughly
  chopped
2 tablespoons maraschino syrup
⅔ cup Basic Bombe Mousse
  (page 71)

Line a chilled 1.2 litre/2 pint/5 cup mould with the softened raspberry ice cream. Cover and freeze until firm.

Remove the mould from the freezer and spread the softened vanilla ice cream in an even layer over the raspberry ice cream. Cover and freeze until firm.

Add the remaining ingredients to the basic bombe mixture and fold lightly together. Fill the centre of the mould with this mixture, cover and freeze until firm.
Serves 8 to 12

Ice Cream Birthday Cake

Choose ice cream mixtures which do not freeze too hard, the mousses, soufflés and still-freeze recipes, for the filling. Tidy up the assembled cake when it is frozen fairly hard before decorating with the icing.

METRIC/IMPERIAL

For the cake
4 eggs
100 g/4 oz caster sugar
75 g/3 oz plain flour
1 teaspoon baking powder
pinch of salt
For the filling
1 litre/1 ³⁄4 pints Iced Raspberry
  Soufflé (page 34)
1 litre/1 ³⁄4 pints Lemon Ice Cream
  (page 28)
For the icing
450 ml/³⁄4 pint double cream
50 g/2 oz icing sugar
food colourings

AMERICAN

For the cake
4 eggs
¹⁄2 cup superfine sugar
³⁄4 cup all-purpose flour
1 teaspoon baking powder
pinch of salt
For the filling
4 ¹⁄4 cups Iced Raspberry Soufflé
  (page 34)
4 ¹⁄4 cups Lemon Ice Cream
  (page 28)
For the icing
2 cups heavy cream
¹⁄2 cup confectioners' sugar
food colourings

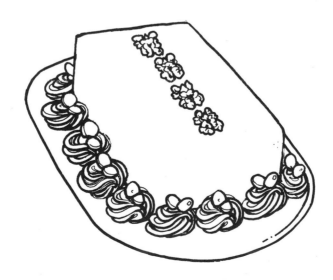

To make the sponge layers, beat the eggs until they are very pale and thick. Still beating, gradually add the sugar and continue beating until the whisk leaves a trail.

Sift together the flour, baking powder and salt and fold them quickly and lightly into the egg mixture.

Pour the mixture into a loose-bottomed 25 cm/10 inch square cake tin, lined with non-stick baking parchment.

Bake the cake in a preheated moderately hot oven (200°C/400°F/ Gas Mark 6) for about 15 minutes, or until it is lightly browned on top.

Remove the cake from the oven and cool for a minute or two before turning out on to a wire rack. Peel off the paper and leave the cake to cool. When it is quite cold, split it carefully into three layers, using a serrated-edged knife.

To assemble the cake place the first sponge layer on a square cake base or plate and spread it evenly with the softened Raspberry Soufflé mixture. Top with the second sponge layer, cover and freeze until firm.

Remove from the freezer and spread evenly with the softened Lemon Ice Cream, top with the third layer of sponge, cover and freeze until firm. When the cake is firm, neaten the sides with a long straight knife dipped in water.

To ice the cake, whip the cream in a chilled bowl until it forms soft peaks. Add the icing sugar and continue beating until it forms soft peaks.

Use about half the cream to 'ice' the top and sides of the cake. Return the cake to the freezer until the cream hardens.

Divide the remaining cream between three small bowls and tint each portion with a different food colour.

Using plastic or greaseproof paper piping bags, decorate the cake with piped cream. Return the cake to the freezer and open (flash) freeze then wrap for storage.

Ripen the cake in the refrigerator for about an hour before serving.

Serves about 20 children

Coupes

Iced coupes, sometimes called sundaes or parfaits, are deliciously festive looking composite sweets based on ice cream. The ices, which may be sherbets, sorbets or ice creams are served in tall glasses or ice cups and are lavishly dressed with fruits, syrups or sauces, Chantilly Cream and nuts or sugared flower petals. The variations are endless, so make up your own recipes with all the flavours you like best.

Blackcurrant Coupe	Sugared blackcurrants, Vanilla Ice Cream, Blackcurrant Sorbet, crème de cassis or Blackcurrant Syrup and Chantilly Cream.
Cherry Coupe	Cherries soaked in syrup or brandy, Cherry Ice Cream, Vanilla Ice Cream and Chantilly Cream decorated with halved fresh Cherries.
Coffee Coupe	Coffee Ice Cream, Dark Chocolate Sauce, Cappucino Ice Cream, Tia Maria or more chocolate sauce, and Chantilly Cream decorated with grated chocolate or toasted nuts.
Praline Coupe	Praline Ice Cream, Caramel Syrup, Caramel Ice Cream and Chantilly Cream decorated with toasted almonds.
Strawberry Coupe	Sugared fresh strawberries, Lemon Ice Cream, Strawberry Sauce, Strawberry Ice Cream or Sorbet, and Chantilly Cream decorated with fresh Strawberries or toasted almonds.
Caribbean Coupe	Fresh pineapple chunks soaked in white rum and sugar, Pineapple Ice Cream, and Chantilly Cream.
Butterscotch Coupe	Caramelized walnuts, Butterscotch Ice Cream, Vanilla Ice Cream, Butterscotch Sauce and Chantilly Cream decorated with walnut halves.
Chocolate Fudge Sundae	Chocolate Ice Cream, Vanilla Ice Cream, Chocolate Fudge Sauce, toasted hazelnuts and Chantilly Cream.
Honey Melon Coupe	Melon and Ginger Ice Cream, Melon Sorbet, Honey Sauce and Chantilly Cream decorated with crystallized ginger.

ICE CREAM BIRTHDAY CAKE *(page 74)*

SAUCES AND WAFERS

Dark Chocolate Sauce

METRIC/IMPERIAL	AMERICAN
100 g/4 oz plain chocolate	*4 squares semi-sweet chocolate*
120 ml/4 fl oz golden syrup	*½ cup light corn syrup*
2 tablespoons rum or brandy	*2 tablespoons rum or brandy*

Put all the ingredients in a small bowl and heat over a pan of simmering water. Stir until the chocolate has melted and the mixture is smooth and shiny.

Serve hot. Alternatively, allow the sauce to cool before storing in a covered container.

Makes about 250 ml/8 fl oz/1 cup

Variation:
Substitute strong coffee, evaporated milk or orange juice for the rum or brandy.

Strawberry Sauce

METRIC/IMPERIAL
225 g/8 oz strawberries
juice of 1 orange
50 g/2 oz caster sugar

AMERICAN
1 ½ cups strawberries
juice of 1 orange
¼ cup superfine sugar

Hull, wash and dry the strawberries. Rub them through a fine sieve, or process them lightly in a blender and strain the purée. Mix the strawberry purée with the orange juice and sugar and refrigerate for at least an hour to develop the flavour.

Store in a covered container in the refrigerator.

Makes about 250 ml/8 fl oz/1 cup

Variation:
Any other soft fruits may be used.

Honey Sauce

Use strongly scented clear honey for this sauce.

METRIC/IMPERIAL
120 ml/4 fl oz clear honey
120 ml/4 fl oz single cream
2 tablespoons whisky (optional)

AMERICAN
½ cup clear honey
½ cup single cream
2 tablespoons whisky (optional)

Put all the ingredients in a small bowl and heat the mixture over a pan of simmering water. Stir the sauce until it is hot and well blended.

Serve hot, or cool the sauce and store it in a covered container.

Makes about 250 ml/8 fl oz/1 cup

Butterscotch Sauce

METRIC/IMPERIAL
50 g/2 oz butter
100 g/4 oz soft brown sugar
pinch of salt
150 ml/¼ pint evaporated milk

AMERICAN
¼ cup butter
⅔ cup soft brown sugar
pinch of salt
⅔ cup evaporated milk

Put the butter, sugar and salt in a small, heavy based saucepan and heat gently until the sugar just begins to caramelize.

Add the evaporated milk and stir until the mixture is well blended.

Serve immediately, or cool the sauce, stirring from time to time.

Makes about 250 ml/8 fl oz/1 cup

Marmalade Sauce

Use dark marmalade, or apricot, cherry or other jams to make variations.

METRIC/IMPERIAL
100 g/4 oz marmalade
120 ml/4 fl oz water
2 tablespoons brandy (optional)

AMERICAN
½ cup marmalade
½ cup water
2 tablespoons brandy (optional)

Put all the ingredients in a small, heavy based pan and heat gently, stirring constantly, until the mixture is well blended.

Strain and serve hot, or cool the strained sauce and store in a covered container.

Makes about 250 ml/8 fl oz/1 cup

BLACKCURRANT COUPE *(page 76)*

Chantilly Cream

METRIC/IMPERIAL	AMERICAN
3 tablespoons water	3 tablespoons water
300 ml/½ pint double cream, chilled	1¼ cups heavy cream, chilled
1 tablespoon caster sugar	1 tablespoon superfine sugar

Put the water and beaters in a bowl and chill in the freezer until ice crystals begin to form. Add the cream and beat until the cream holds soft peaks. Sprinkle on the sugar, and beat it in very lightly. Use to decorate ices or in coupes or sundaes.
Makes about 600 ml/1 pint/2½ cups

Variation:
Substitute all or part of the water with brandy or liqueurs.

Blackcurrant Syrup

METRIC/IMPERIAL	AMERICAN
225 g/8 oz blackcurrants	2 cups blackcurrants
100 g/4 oz granulated sugar	½ cup sugar
250 ml/8 fl oz water	1 cup water

Top and tail the blackcurrants and put them in a pan with the sugar and water. Bring slowly to the boil, lower the heat and simmer for about 5 minutes. Strain the syrup through a fine sieve lined with muslin (cheesecloth). Cool the syrup and store in a covered container.
Makes about 250 ml/8 fl oz/1 cup

Variation:
Substitute raspberries for the blackcurrants.

Caramel Syrup

METRIC/IMPERIAL
225 g/8 oz granulated sugar
300 ml/½ pint water

AMERICAN
1 cup sugar
1¼ cups water

Put the sugar in a small, heavy based saucepan with 4 tablespoons/ ¼ cup of the water. Slowly heat together until the sugar has dissolved, then raise the heat and boil the mixture until the sugar caramelizes to a deep golden brown.

Take the pan off the heat and carefully add the rest of the water. Stir with a wooden spoon until the caramel has dissolved, heating the syrup again if necessary to dissolve it all.

Makes about 250 ml/8 fl oz/1 cup

Geneva Wafers

METRIC/IMPERIAL	AMERICAN
75 g/3 oz butter	*⅓ cup butter*
75 g/3 oz caster sugar	*⅓ cup superfine sugar*
2 eggs, beaten	*2 eggs, beaten*
75 g/3 oz plain flour, sifted	*¾ cup all-purpose flour, sifted*

Cream the butter, add the sugar and beat until the mixture is pale and light. Beat in alternate spoonfuls of egg and flour until both are incorporated. Bake as below then cool on a wire rack and store in an airtight container.

To make flat, round wafers, drop small teaspoonsful of the mixture on to greased baking sheets, spacing them well apart. Bake in a preheated slow oven (150°C/300°F, Gas Mark 2) for about 30 minutes, or until pale golden.

To make *langues de chat,* pipe the mixture, using a plain nozzle, in 5 cm/2 inch lengths on to prepared baking sheets, spacing them well apart. Bake for about 30 minutes, or until pale golden.

To make cones, drop tablespoonsful of the mixture on to prepared baking sheets, spacing them well apart. Bake them for about 20 minutes, then remove the partly cooked wafers from the oven and roll them round greased cornet moulds. Return them to the oven for 10 to 15 minutes to crisp.

Makes at least 35, depending on size.

From left: PEACH MELBA YOGURT ICE *(page 50)*, GREENGAGE YOGURT ICE CREAM *(page 51)*, HONEY YOGURT ICE *(page 51)*, RASPBERRY YOGURT ICE *(page 50)*

Chocolate Fudge Sauce

METRIC/IMPERIAL
50 g/2 oz plain chocolate
120 ml/4 fl oz sweetened condensed milk
4 tablespoons water
25 g/1 oz butter

AMERICAN
2 squares semi-sweet chocolate
½ cup sweetened condensed milk
¼ cup water
2 tablespoons butter

Put the chocolate and condensed milk in a small bowl and heat over a pan of simmering water. Stir until the chocolate has melted, then beat in the water and butter.

Serve hot.

Makes about 250 ml/8 fl oz/1 cup

Toasted Nut Toppings

To toast almonds: spread about 50 g/2 oz/½ cup of blanched, slivered almonds on a baking sheet and toast in a preheated moderate oven (160°C/325°F, Gas Mark 3) for about 12 minutes, or until they are lightly browned.

To toast hazelnuts: spread about 50 g/2 oz/⅓ cup of shelled hazelnuts on a baking sheet and toast in a preheated moderate oven (160°C/325°F, Gas Mark 3) for 15 to 20 minutes, or until the centres are a pale biscuit colour. Cool the nuts, rub off the skins and chop finely.

To caramelize walnuts: heat 50 g/2 oz/¼ cup caster (superfine) sugar in a small, heavy based saucepan until it has melted and turned a rich golden brown. Pour the caramel over 50 g/2 oz/½ cup shelled walnuts spread on a sheet of greased foil. When the caramel has set, crush the praline in a mortar, or use a food processor to reduce it to small chips.

Ratafias

METRIC/IMPERIAL	AMERICAN
5 egg whites	*5 egg whites*
225 g/8 oz ground almonds	*2 cups ground almonds*
350 g/12 oz caster sugar	*1 ½ cups superfine sugar*
1 teaspoon almond or ratafia essence	*1 teaspoon almond or ratafia extract*

In a large bowl, whisk the egg whites until they form stiff peaks. Fold in the ground almonds, sugar and flavouring; mix well together to form a soft, sticky dough.

Line several baking sheets with rice paper or non-stick baking parchment and pipe small mounds of the mixture about 1.5 cm/ ¾ inch diameter, on to the paper. Use a plain nozzle and space them well apart. Bake the ratafias in a preheated slow oven (150°C/300°F, Gas Mark 2) for about 45 minutes, or until they are a pale pinkish brown.

Transfer the biscuits (cookies) still on the paper, to a wire cooling rack. When they are quite cold, trim away the excess rice paper, or peel off the baking parchment, and store the ratafias in an airtight container.

Makes about 100

Lemon Bourbons

METRIC/IMPERIAL
3 eggs
225 g/8 oz caster sugar
250 g/9 oz plain flour, sifted
pinch of salt
grated rind of 1 lemon

AMERICAN
3 eggs
1 cup superfine sugar
2¼ cups all-purpose flour, sifted
pinch of salt
grated rind of 1 lemon

In a large bowl beat the eggs with 200 g/7 oz/1 scant cup of the sugar, until the mixture is very pale and the whisk leaves a trail. Mix together the flour, salt and lemon rind. Fold the dry ingredients into the egg mixture. Spoon the mixture into a large piping bag fitted with a plain nozzle.

Pipe small mounds or fingers of the mixture on to baking sheets which have been well greased and floured or lined with non-stick baking parchment. Dust the biscuits (cookies) with the remaining sugar and set them aside to dry for about 1 hour.

Tap off the excess sugar and bake the biscuits (cookies) in a preheated hot oven (200°C/400°F, Gas Mark 6) for about 10 minutes, or until they are very lightly coloured. Cool slightly before peeling off the baking parchment, if used, and transferring to a wire cooling rack. When they are cold, store the bourbons in an airtight container. Serve with fruit ices.
Makes about 75

From centre: RATAFIAS *(page 87)*, GENEVA WAFERS *(page 84)*,
LEMON BOURBONS, VANILLA WAFERS *(page 90)*

Vanilla Wafers

METRIC/IMPERIAL
100 g/4 oz butter
50 g/2 oz caster sugar
1 egg, beaten
½ teaspoon vanilla essence
75 g/3 oz plain flour, sifted

AMERICAN
½ cup butter
¼ cup superfine sugar
1 egg, beaten
½ teaspoon vanilla extract
¾ cup all-purpose flour, sifted

Cream the butter, add the sugar and beat until the mixture is pale and light. Slowly add the beaten egg mixed with the vanilla and continue beating until the mixture is fluffy. Add the flour and mix until well blended.

Drop teaspoonsful of the dough on to baking sheets which have been lined with non-stick baking parchment or been well-greased. Space the wafers well apart to allow for spreading. Bake in a preheated moderately hot oven (190°C/375°F, Gas Mark 5) for about 15 minutes or until golden brown at the edges.

Cool the wafers on a wire rack before storing in an airtight container. Serve with most ice creams.
Makes about 90

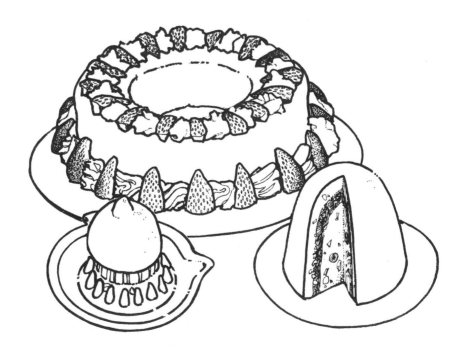

INDEX

INDEX